Parents' Guide to THE NATIONAL CURRICULUM in [illegible] Schools

KEY STAGE 3

David Bell

Charles Letts & Co Ltd
London, Edinburgh & New York

First published 1991
by Charles Letts & Co. Ltd
Diary House, Borough Road, London SE1 1DW

Photographs: Sally and Richard Greenhill
Illustrations: Bee Willey
Cover photograph: David Johnson

Editorial team: Angela Royal, Chris Norris
Design team: Anne Davison, Keith Anderson

Acknowledgements

The author and publishers wish to thank the following schools and colleges for their co-operation in researching the case-study:

Berry Hill High School, Stoke-on-Trent
Manormead School (Special), Abbey Wood
Thames Polytechnic, School of Education (Avery Hill Campus)
Thomas Tallis School, Greenwich

They would also like to extend special thanks to Stoke Newington School and to Narelle Holland, the school's Head of Resources.

ISBN 0 85097 926 9

British Library CIP statement

A CIP catalogue record for this book
is available from the British Library.

Printed and bound in Great Britain by
Charles Letts (Scotland) Ltd

Contents

Introduction

This book provides a short but comprehensive guide to all aspects of your child's secondary education between the ages of 11 and 14, (key stage 3 of the National Curriculum). It also describes the preparations that have to be made before your child starts secondary school.

Throughout, the partnership between parents, pupils and teachers is stressed. Your child will be happier, and will perform more effectively at school, when you take an active interest in all that goes on. Also, teachers can do work with more confidence when they have the backing of informed and interested parents.

Recently, secondary schools have undergone major changes which are reflected in this book. The headings covered are:

— Leaving primary school;
— Choosing a secondary school;
— Introduction to the National Curriculum;
— The National Curriculum core subjects;
— The National Curriculum foundation subjects;
— Assessment;
— The wider life of a secondary school;
— Monitoring your child's progress;
— The management of a school;
— Getting involved;
— Moving on;
— Case study.

All the recent reforms should reflect the needs of pupils. It is the schoolchildren who are the focus of this parents' guide to secondary education at key stage 3.

Leaving primary school

Most primary schools have fewer than 400 pupils. Imagine then, the culture shock for your child as they leave primary school and enter a large secondary school which could have over 1000 pupils. They are exchanging the intimate atmosphere of a small primary school, where they were the senior pupils, for an unfamiliar environment which can appear impersonal and hostile. Also, most eleven-year old children have been in a class which had the one teacher for most subjects. At secondary school, pupils can have up to ten teachers and move from classroom to classroom. Secondary education can seem much more formal than primary education. This can be unsettling for new pupils.

However, many secondary schools have recognized these difficulties and have introduced ways of making the transition easier. These include:

— Final year primary children visiting the secondary school for a day or even a week of timetabled lessons.

— Secondary teachers coming to work in the primary school to gain a better understanding of the children's work.

— Regular meetings between primary and secondary staff to discuss in detail the children who will be changing school.

— Better records being passed between primary and secondary schools so that the secondary teachers' background information about their new pupils is improved.

Some secondary schools have also radically altered the way in which first-year pupils are taught. They have tried to keep primary class groups (or groups of friends) together for most of the school week. A form teacher (or tutor) has regular contact with these classes. This usually forms part of a wider pastoral system which all secondary schools have, irrespective of their arrangements for first-year pupils. In addition, children go through adolescent changes at puberty. This mixture of rapid psychological and physical change can be a volatile experience. Schools are well-used to dealing with pupils at different stages of development. Parents can assist their children's educational and development in these ways:

— **Be realistic** Don't have unrealistic expectations of your child which can never be met. However able your child is, they will not perform to the best of their ability if under constant pressure. Yet . . .

— **Be challenging** Encourage your child in every way possible and provide opportunities for them to participate in all aspects of school life. Find out from your child what homework they have to do and provide the right conditions at home for them do this work such as a quiet room for studying.

— **Be sensitive** Adolescents need your time and attention. However, sometimes they need to be left alone to find their own way. It is important for you to take an interest in their education but it will not be the same as when your child was at primary school.

Choosing a secondary school

The majority of parents will opt to send their child to the local secondary school. There are advantages in doing this. It is usually more convenient for the child, as it is unlikely to involve long journeys. It also means that your child will attend the same school as friends from primary school and the local neighbourhood. However, an increasing number of parents are exercising their right to send their child to a school further afield provided that there are places elsewhere. If a school is oversubscribed, not all parents' wishes will be granted. When this occurs, account is taken of other factors such as siblings already at a school or the distance to the school (relative to other local schools). A school is not allowed to refuse admission to a child provided there are spaces available.

So what are the options? Each Local Education Authority (LEA) is responsible for providing education in their designated area. Thus patterns of organization vary from LEA to LEA. The most common provision is:

— 'All through' schools for 11-18 year olds

— Schools for 11-16 year olds and sixth form or tertiary colleges for 16 year old students and over.

— Middle schools for 8-12 or 9-13 year olds and high schools for 12-18 or 13-18 year olds.

The vast majority of LEAs have organized secondary education along comprehensive lines. This means that pupils of all abilities attend the same school. In some places, selection at age 11 remains with a small percentage of pupils attending grammar schools and the rest attending comprehensive secondary schools.

If you have a choice of school, what should you be looking for? It is very important to telephone the school to arrange a visit. That first phone call can be vital in creating your first impression of the school. Are you welcomed to visit at any time? Is your child invited to accompany you? Are you discouraged from coming on your own and encouraged to come with a larger group? Are you dissuaded from coming at all? Are you given helpful directions to the school and sent any literature, such as the school prospectus, in advance of your visit? Are you given the Head Teacher's name if you do not already have it? The very best schools will welcome known and prospective parents alike, whether they be on the telephone, or making a personal call.

So what questions might you ask yourself about a school?

Outside the school

— Is the school well cared for generally?
— Do the gardens and surrounding grounds look tidy?
— Is there graffiti on or around the building?
— How do pupils behave when moving in and out of the building?
— If you speak to local people, what do they say about the behaviour of the pupils?
— Is there friendly and welcoming signpost directing you to the main entrance?

Inside the school

— What is your first impression? Is the school bright and clean with interesting collections of students' work on display by the main entrance?
— Are you, and your child, welcomed in a friendly way and are you made to feel at home?
— Who has been assigned to host your visit to the school?
— Are you kept waiting and, if so, does the Head Teacher or host provide an explanation?

The aims and objectives of the school

— Does the Head Teacher have a clear idea of the educational aims of the school?
— Are you given some explanation of the range of subjects on offer and how this alters as pupils progress through the school?
— Are you made to feel that the school is part of a wider community with a range of other activities going on?
— Are you, and your child, made to feel that you could make a positive contribution to the school?
— Does the school have a clear but simple set of rules?

Around the classrooms

— Are you given the opportunity to see around the school? If so, by whom? If not, why not?
— When you visit classrooms, does the Head Teacher introduce you personally to members of staff?
— Are you given an opportunity to see examples of pupils' work? Is it of a high standard? Is it marked?
— Are the classrooms (laboratories, music room, etc) tidy and well organized?
— What can you tell about the relationships between teachers and pupils and between the pupils themselves?
— Are you taken to see classes of different ages?
— Are you shown a whole range of subjects being taught? Are there any obvious omissions?
— What is the school's policy on homework?
— How do pupils move around inside the building? Is it purposeful and orderly?

It is important to say something about public examinations because these are the measures by which schools are often compared. All schools are required to publish certain results. These can act as a useful indicator of what the school is achieving. However, it is misleading to make simple 'raw' comparisons between schools in widely different catchment areas. If this information is provided, it is much more useful to compare schools serving similar communities and to measure an individual school's progress over a number of years.

The relationship between pupil and teacher is vital for success

All schools must provide details of the GCSE examinations and GCE A-Level examinations held the previous year giving:

— The number of pupils, in the appropriate year group, who attained each grade for all subject areas;

— The total number of pupils in each of the appropriate year groups.

It is important to ask about the schools policy for entering pupils for public examinations as some schools encourage only the 'near certainties' to enter. In addition, you might want to ask about other kinds of educational achievement, or where pupils go when they leave the school.

Examination results are important and you will want to feel confident that the school of your choice is likely to provide your child with a reasonable chance of success. Yet, results alone do not necessarily indicate the ideal school. Although schools differ in many ways, the most important aspect of a school is its ethos, or atmosphere. This is very difficult to describe but if you visit a number of schools, you will have a different 'feeling' about each one. Ultimately, you and your child need to make a decision that takes into consideration all the relevant factors. It is a vital decision and it deserves serious time and effort even if you eventually decide on the local school.

Introduction to the National Curriculum

All pupils in state schools from the age of five are now required to follow the National Curriculum. This was introduced by the Conservative government, in September 1989, following the passing of the Education Reform Act 1988. It came after a period of time when there had been considerable discussion about educational standards. It was argued by the government (and broadly accepted by other political parties) that that National Curriculum would have three advantages:

1 It would ensure that all children in the country would follow the same set of subjects in school; guaranteeing that the curriculum was no longer 'left to chance'.

2 By setting attainment targets or benchmarks that children had to reach by certain ages, it would ensure that teaching became more purposeful and that better use of time was made by both teachers and pupils.

3 Parents could move their children around the country and know that schools would be following a broadly similar curriculum. Thus, discontinuity to these children's education would be minimized.

Subjects

The National Curriculum prescribes the following subjects for pupils aged between 11 and 14.

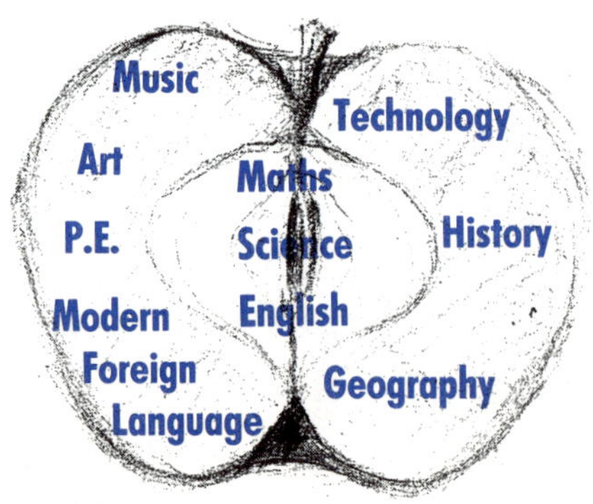

The curriculum is divided into the core subjects of maths, English and science. In addition, there are foundation subjects of: technology; history; geography; a modern foreign language; music; art; and physical education. Welsh is a core subject in Welsh-speaking schools and a foundation subject in all other Welsh schools. Pupils must also receive religious education and a daily act of collective worship.

The content of each of these subjects is or will be outlined in documents which have been issued to all schools in the country. These have two major elements:

Attainment Targets What children should know and be able to do at each stage;

Programmes of Study What children should be taught in order to reach the attainment targets.

To make it easier to understand, the work in each subject is parcelled up into profile components, or groups of related attainment targets (ATs). For the core subjects, the profile components (PCs) are listed below:

PC1	PC2
Number Algebra Measures	Shape Space Handling data

Maths

PC1	PC2
Exploration of science	Knowledge and understanding of science

Science

PC1	PC2	PC3
Speaking and listening	Reading	Writing

English

The National Curriculum does not specify how individual subjects should be taught or how lessons should be organized. Additionally, the National Curriculum does not specify how much teaching time should be given to each subject, although the attainment targets and programmes of study do reflect general assumptions about the amount of time appropriate for teaching the core and foundation subjects. For example, it is possible that your child's timetable will not actually include the word 'Technology'. However, the requirements of the National Curriculum could be met through other subjects, such as: craft, design and technology; home economics; and information technology. The organization of the curriculum is a matter for individual Head Teachers to decide.

Assessment

The National Curriculum places great emphasis on assessment that charts pupils' progress through the various subjects. All of the subjects are divided into ten levels and pupils are assessed continuously by teachers with more formal assessments at certain stages. These formal assessments are called Standard Assessment Tasks (SATs). The arrangement for assessment are discussed in more detail later in this book.

Key stages

The old terminology of first year, second year etc, will slowly disappear. The National Curriculum has brought in a different way of describing the year groups.

In addition, these year groups are classified into key stages. At the end of each key stage, important formal assessments will be undertaken by the children. In some ways, the old distinctions between primary and secondary will become less important in academic terms, because your child's education will now continue

Age of the majority of pupils at the end of the academic year	New description	Abbreviation
12	Year 7	Y 7
13	Year 8	Y 8
14	Year 9	Y 9
15	Year 10	Y 10
16	Year 11	Y 11
17	Year 12	Y 12
18	Year 13	Y 13

uninterrupted from ages 5 to 16. However, the transition from key stage 2 (end of primary) to key stage 3 (beginning of secondary) does mark a move towards more formal work within individual subjects of the curriculum.

Age of children	Key stage
5-7	1
7-11	2
11-14	3
14-16	4

Introducing the National Curriculum

	Pupils aged 11 years beginning of key stage 3	Pupils aged 14 years beginning of key stage 4*
1989	Mathematics Science	
1990	English Technology	
1991	History Geography	
1992	Modern Language Art Music PE	Mathematics Science English
1993		Technology
1994		History Geography
1995		Modern Language Art Music PE

* estimated dates (see page 13)

The National Curriculum is a major change to education in this country which cannot be introduced overnight. The timetable on page 12 sets out when the requirements of the National Curriculum for different subject areas will be introduced. In the meantime, schools have to ensure that all subjects are taught for a reasonable amount of time before their formal introduction into the National Curriculum.

The timetable and structure of key stage 4 are still under discussion. As yet, there are no firm decisions about the National Curriculum on offer to 14 to 16 year olds. However, it is likely that pupils will not have to take all ten foundation subjects. Key stage 4 will have to mould into the existing GCSE system (see page 30).

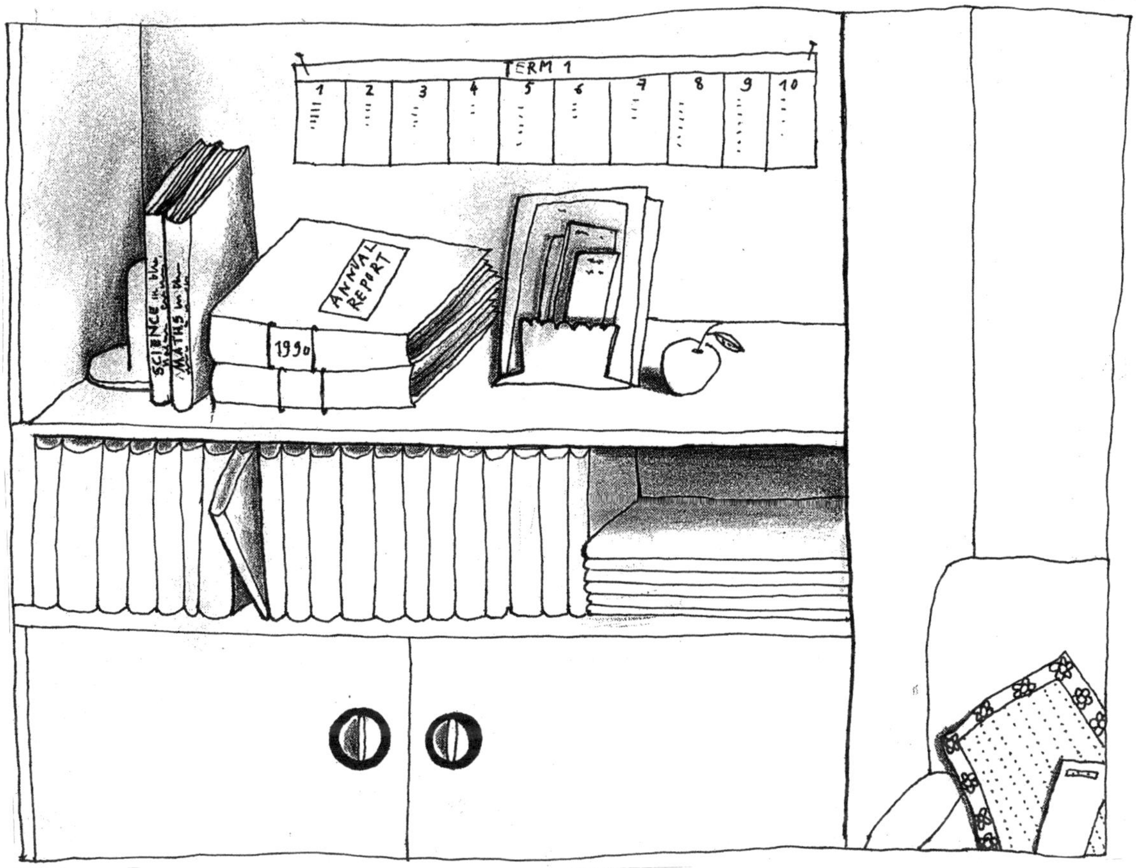

The National Curriculum core subjects

The core subjects: mathematics

Pupils' work in mathematics will be divided into two profile components in the National Curriculum. These indicate the range of activities that pupils will undertake between the ages of 11 and 14.

Mathematics Profile Component 1

Knowledge, skills, understanding and use of number, algebra and measures

AT1: Using and applying mathematics in number, algebra and measurement.

AT2: Understand number and number notation.

AT3: Understand number operations (the four rules).

AT4: Estimate and approximate in number.

AT5: Patterns and relationships in number and algebra.

AT6: Algebraic functions and formulae.

AT7: Algebraic representations in graph forms.

AT8: Measures.

Mathematics Profile Component 2

Knowledge, skills, understanding and use of shape and space and data handling.

AT9: Using and applying the mathematics of shape, space and handling data.

AT10: Shape and space: two and three dimensional shapes.

AT11: Shape and space: location and transformations.

AT12: Collection, recording and processing data.

AT13: Representation and interpretation of data.

AT14: Probabilities.

The National Curriculum in mathematics at key stage 3 offers a wide range of experience to pupils. It recognizes that mathematics is an important subject in its own right and also a means by which other subjects and disciplines can be more thoroughly understood. There is an underlying emphasis throughout, on pupils starting to think and work as mathematicians: designing tasks; choosing materials; following a chain of mathematical reasoning; testing generalizations and simple hypotheses; and presenting findings. A number of schools now use individualized work programmes in mathematics which allow pupils to progress at their own pace and to use a range of mathematical skills.

The National Curriculum assumes that pupils will be doing a significant amount of practical number work in the first year or so at secondary school. For instance, using fractions and percentages, calculating using ratios and working with decimals are all important numerical skills. Throughout, there is a strong emphasis on approximation and estimation so that pupils are able to check whether their calculations 'look' correct. This is very important as calculators have become more important working tools in mathematics. The National Curriculum recognizes the importance of calculators but only allows them to complement existing knowledge, not to supplant it. Number work then develops into working with positive integers and prime numbers. Pupils also gain experience of working with negative numbers.

In algebra, pupils build on the work they have been doing at primary school. Children learn how to find possible rules for generating sequences. Simple equations are also introduced and developed. Algebra takes up an increasing amount of time over the next couple of years at secondary school and the National Curriculum recognizes this shift of emphasis. For instance: exploring number patterns generated by a computer; gaining confidence in the use of symbols; and drawing and interpreting straight line graphs all form part of the work in algebra. By the time a pupil is 14, they will be using a range of formulae and functions, manipulating simple algebraic expressions and understanding the relationship between powers and roots of numbers.

Practical work in measuring shape and space is likely to have formed an important part of your child's primary education. This emphasis continues at the early stages of the secondary school, although there is now a stronger emphasis on the underlying mathematical principles. For example, the angle and symmetry properties of shapes are examined in more detail. General principles, such as Pythagoras' Theorem, are used to understand right-angled triangles. In measurement work, greater emphasis is placed on carrying out more complex calculations using formulae, (e.g. to find out the area of a shape).

The National Curriculum has increased the importance of data handling. There is a clear recognition that pupils need to present findings, using mathematical skills, in the interpretation of data. Pupils will be devising questionnaires, surveying opinions and presenting their findings in a variety of statistical ways. They will be examining probabilities and checking frequencies and the outcomes of events. This kind of work recognizes that pupils need to become skilled over a wide range of skills beyond the four number operations.

The teaching of mathematics has undergone many changes in recent years. Reference has already been made to individualized learning approaches. In addition, teachers are likely to encourage co-operative working within mathematical projects in which a topic or theme is looked at in depth for a period of time. Textbooks remain important but it is recognized that pupils need to learn and practice skills in a variety of contexts. The National Curriculum in mathematics reinforces this point.

The core subjects: English

The National Curriculum in English at key stage 3 has five attainment targets grouped into three profile components.

English Profile Component 1

Knowledge, skills and understanding in speaking and listening.

> AT1: Understanding of the spoken word and the ability to speak and listen effectively in a variety of contexts.

English Profile Component 2

Knowledge, skills and understanding in reading.

> AT2: Ability to read, understand and respond to all types of writing as well as the ability to retrieve information.

English Profile Component 3

Knowledge, skills and understanding in writing.

> AT3: Writing.
>
> AT4: Spelling.
>
> AT5: Presentation.

The National Curriculum envisages an extremely broad English curriculum. Reflecting good practice in the teaching of English, it recognizes the need for pupils to be confident speakers and careful listeners. The individual contributions of all pupils are valued, with lessons giving many opportunities for children to give instructions to others, prepare and present a well-argued case, or solve practical problems related to the school/wider community. The ability to listen goes hand in hand with the ability to speak. Pupils need to show sensitivity to the points of view of others. Children also need to use spoken language in formal contexts. The National Curriculum recognizes the importance of using texts or scripts. Pupils need to distinguish between the uses of English in different contexts. A pupil at key stage 3 may well use non-standard English in some contexts but should use standard English in other contexts where appropriate. Throughout key stage 3, the value of spoken language in personal presentation and wider community life is recognized. Pupils are learning to use language for life.

Teenagers have many different views about reading. For some, becoming engrossed in a good book is one of life's greatest pleasures. For others, reading is something to be avoided or channelled into particular subjects such as sport, or the television pages of a newspaper. The National Curriculum introduces pupils to a wide range of important literature from Shakespeare to 20th century writers. By this stage of their school career, pupils need to be reading literature that is not specifically written for young people. They also have to become sensitive to language and its use in different contexts. Ideally, they will acquire a passion for words, how they are used, and how their use can change over time. Throughout, reading for pleasure is stressed. Most secondary schools have good library facilities for pupils to enjoy. Yet, the importance of reading for information is not overlooked; pupils need to know how to use reference books and interrogate computer databases. They also need to skim and scan the materials they read. The National Curriculum emphasizes the importance of such skills being taught. Some people might be surprised to see that *grammar* does not appear as a separate category within the National Curriculum. However, at key stage 3 there is a strong emphasis placed on the way that sentences, and longer pieces of writing, are constructed. The emphasis is on the use of writing in practical contexts and on how different styles of writing demand different forms of language, (e.g. scientific writing is usually characterized by writing in the third person). Pupils also need to demonstrate that they are aware of different audiences that they can write for. For instance, the style of writing for an intimate letter is very different to that of a formal essay.

The National Curriculum in English acknowledges that language crosses into all other areas of the curriculum. For instance, as pupils write history essays they are learning about structuring their writing to present a case, or further an argument. Equally, as they study modern languages they can see how English words have a number of different origins. Overall, the emphasis is on language for communication, in all its forms. Secondary schools would not feel they had succeeded unless their pupils developed the skills of good communication.

The core subjects: science

Laboratory work is a new experience for many pupils

Science becomes a vital part of the National Curriculum with it being one of the core subjects. The National Curriculum in science is structured in a slightly different way from the other two core subjects. There are two profile components but the first one only has one attainment target. This describes the scientific processes needed to investigate the attainment targets within the science curriculum.

Science Profile Component 1

Exploration of science, communication and the application of knowledge and understanding.

AT1: Exploration of science.

Science Profile Component 2

Knowledge and understanding of science, communication and the applications and implications of science.

> AT2: The variety of life.
>
> AT3: Processes of life.
>
> AT4: Genetics and evolution.
>
> AT5: Human influences on the Earth.
>
> AT6: Types and uses of materials.
>
> AT7: Making new materials.
>
> AT8: Explaining how materials behave.
>
> AT9: Earth and atmosphere.
>
> AT10: Forces.
>
> AT11: Electricity and magnetism.
>
> AT12: The scientific aspects of information technology including microelectronics.
>
> AT13: Energy.
>
> AT14: Sound and Music.
>
> AT15: Using light and electromagnetic radiation.
>
> AT16: The Earth in space.
>
> AT17: The nature of science.

For many youngsters, science is a particularly exciting subject at secondary school. For the first time, in most cases, they have the opportunity to work regularly in purpose-built laboratories being taught by specialist teachers. The National Curriculum stresses the importance of pupils beginning to think and act as scientists. It emphasizes the skills of attainment target 1 such as: planning safe experiments; selecting appropriate equipment; systematically recording results; and forming generalizations. These skills should be applied across the range of attainment targets in science.

Pupils are expected to gain a lot of scientific knowledge: from investigating the plants and animals in their local environment, through to investigating the properties of magnets and electromagnets and the nature of electric fields. Throughout, there is a strong emphasis on developing their scientific knowledge through familiar contexts. For instance, attainment target 5 includes the study of water, which can be done by monitoring water purity and assessing the presence of soluble and insoluble materials, pH and the oxygen content. Or, in attainment target 7, they can investigate different types of reaction (such as combustion, thermal decomposition, salt formation, corrosion and metal extraction) applying their knowledge to manufacturing processes such as oil fractionation and fermentation.

Work in the physical sciences includes the study of forces. Pupils discover the nature of force and investigate the factors involved in producing and maintaining motion. They also look at the use of simple machines and assess the applications of energy in practical contexts.

The study of sound, music and light all contribute to a wide scientific education at key stage 3. For instance, vision is studied in some detail, as is the behaviour of light. Pupils also learn about the construction of simple optical devices.

Children are usually interested in the place of the Earth in space. This also forms an important part of the science curriculum. For example, they consider changes of day length, as well as looking at the position of the Sun and planets within the solar system. Pupils also need to understand the developmental history of scientific ideas and look in depth at the work of some famous scientists.

The National Curriculum foundation subjects

Although the core subjects of maths, English and science are at the heart of the new curriculum, other subjects, known as the foundation subjects, are also included. These are: technology; history; geography; a modern foreign language; art; music; and physical education.

The structure of the curriculum (in technology, history, geography and the modern foreign language) will be the same as in the core subjects using attainment targets and profile components. The arrangements for art, PE and music are likely to be similar although the curriculum will not be spelled out in such great detail. These three subjects will not be tested nationally at the end of key stage 3.

Detailed guidance is now available to teachers and schools about technology, history, geography and modern foreign languages. Guidelines on the other subjects are likely to become available during 1991.

Technology

Technology is a good example of a subject which schools will deal with in a variety of ways. Some will have a specific subject of that name on the timetable. Others will separate out the IT element. Others still, will teach technology across a range of subjects whilst ensuring that the requirements of the National Curriculum are being met through careful co-ordination. The five attainment targets are: identifying needs and opportunities; generating a design; planning and making; evaluating; and information technology (IT).

The National Curriculum strongly establishes the importance of pupils, at key stage 3, doing their own research which leads to the identification of project tasks for designing and making. They also need to be able to use a variety of materials, such as wood and metal, in a safe and tidy environment. The wider impact of technology is also an important theme for pupils at key stage 3, as they address issues such as market research and setting up a business. They also look at the different historical and cultural factors which have influenced the design of the products we use today. Information technology is an important element of the technology curriculum in which pupils will work with a range of hardware and software, (e.g. computer equipment and programs).

Geography and history

The geography curriculum identifies three particular aspects of geography: geographical skill; geographical areas; and geographical themes.

Geographical skills includes work on Ordnance Survey maps, relief maps and satellite maps. In addition, there is an emphasis on doing field work such as: collecting data; and designing appropriate sketches and diagrams to illustrate a point. At key stage 3, work in geographical areas includes: a study of the pupils' home region; an area within the UK that contrasts with the home region; a country in the EC beyond the UK; a 'developed' area from beyond the EC; a 'developing' country; and a study based on the USA, the USSR or Japan. Pupils also need to be able to pinpoint a number of places on a map. Geographical themes cover a whole range of issues such as: weather; landforms: economic activity; transport and pollution.

The history curriculum has been the subject of intense political and media interest. The emphasis is on British history, although at key stage 3, pupils could be studying the Roman Empire, Western Europe at the time of the Reformation, or the black peoples of the Americas. Historical knowledge and facts are an important element of the curriculum but there is also a great emphasis on historical skills such as: gathering information about the past; understanding different points of view; and presenting historical information, using conventions such as footnotes and appendices.

Modern foreign language

The National Curriculum identifies four main areas of study in modern languages: responding to spoken language; using spoken language; responding to written language; and using written language. The curriculum emphasizes the importance of communication and the use of languages. Pupils will therefore be given every encouragement to work with others in contexts which require the practical use of languages. The National Curriculum specifies that all pupils should be offered an EC language, although schools can offer additional languages. At what age this becomes available for pupils is a matter for individual schools to decide.

Art, music and physical education (PE)

It is generally understood that a good, all-round education has to encompass work in the arts. Secondary schools already ensure that pupils receive some exposure to these areas of the curriculum. It is likely that the National Curriculum will reflect good practice, although there may be greater emphasis on building up skills and knowledge in a more structured way. As the first National Curriculum pupils come through from the primary schools, secondary teachers will be able to build on foundations already established in each of these subjects.

The wider curriculum

Although National Curriculum subjects, or work contributing to the National Curriculum, will make up most of your child's time at secondary school, there are likely to be other elements on the curriculum. For example, personal and social education (PSE) could cover issues such as: health education, careers; and citizenship. There might be a period on the timetable for study skills which could cover: library skills; personal study skills; and working with others.

Secondary schools may also include issues which encompass the whole curriculum, encouraging individual subject teachers to plan them into their work. These could include: equal opportunities; multi-cultural awareness; and economic and industrial understanding. The governments' adivisers on the curriculum, the National Curriculum Council, are encouraging schools to adopt this approach and are providing advice to schools on how it might be achieved. Another important development in schools, particularly for pupils of 14 and above, is the technical and vocational education initiative (TVEI). The emphasis of this scheme is on developing the skills that will be needed for the world of work and different models have been introduced across the country. It is rare for TVEI to appear as a separate element on the curriculum but it influences all subject areas, including elements such as: work experience; setting up mini-enterprises; and developing additional skills in areas such as technology and modern languages.

Assessment

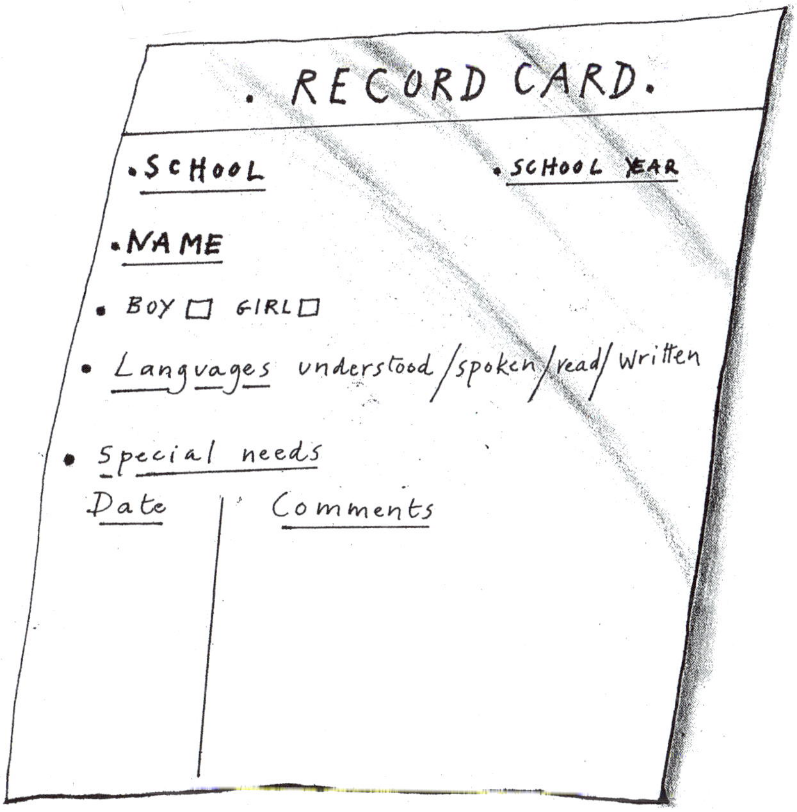

The assessment of pupils' progress is an essential element of the National Curriculum. All teachers assess pupils' progress each day and so assessment is at the heart of teaching. Additionally, most secondary schools have more formal tests, or exams, at different points throughout the school year. These will be tied into the National Curriculum in future. On top of this, there are criteria against which overall progress will be assessed. These are the Attainment Targets covering the main areas of study in each subject. These outline what pupils should normally be expected to know, understand and do at the ages of 7, 11, 14 and 16.

To assist in the assessment of pupils at age 14, there will be Standard Assessment Tasks (SATs). These will cover maths, English and science, with progress in other subjects being monitored in ways left to individual schools to decide. Even with nationally set SATs, teacher assessment will continue to play an important role in making an overall judgment about progress. Pupils' progress will be registered on a ten-point scale for each subject: the national curriculum states what a child must do to progress from one level to the next. For instance, if a thirteen-year old is at level 7, in mathematics Attainment Target 3, this suggests that he, or she, is able to do the following:

— multiply and divide, mentally, single digits of any power of 10 and realize that, with a number less than 1, multiplication has a decreasing effect and division has an increasing effect.
— solve multiplication and division problems involving numbers of any size.
— use the memory and bracket facility of a calculator to plan a calculation and evaluate expressions.

However, when the pupils overall progress is reported at 14, all the attainment targets in this area will be grouped into a profile component of 'number, algebra and measures', to provide an overall level of achievement. When the two profile components in mathematics are taken together, this should represent the pupil's achievement across the whole subject.

Assessment is a central feature of the National Curriculum

The results of these tests will be reported to parents, although individual results will not be widely known. However, all the results from a school will be put together to provide general information to parents about how successful different schools are in delivering the National Curriculum. However, there is some concern, that such comparisons might not be fair, as different schools take children from very different backgrounds. Additionally, a good school is often that way because of other factors which are difficult to measure, such as disciplined pupils or enthusiastic teachers.

Finally, many schools already have adopted a Records of Achievement system which is a way of summarizing their pupils' development and success. Such a system may be used increasingly to provide a broad picture of all aspects of pupil performance, including progress through the National Curriculum.

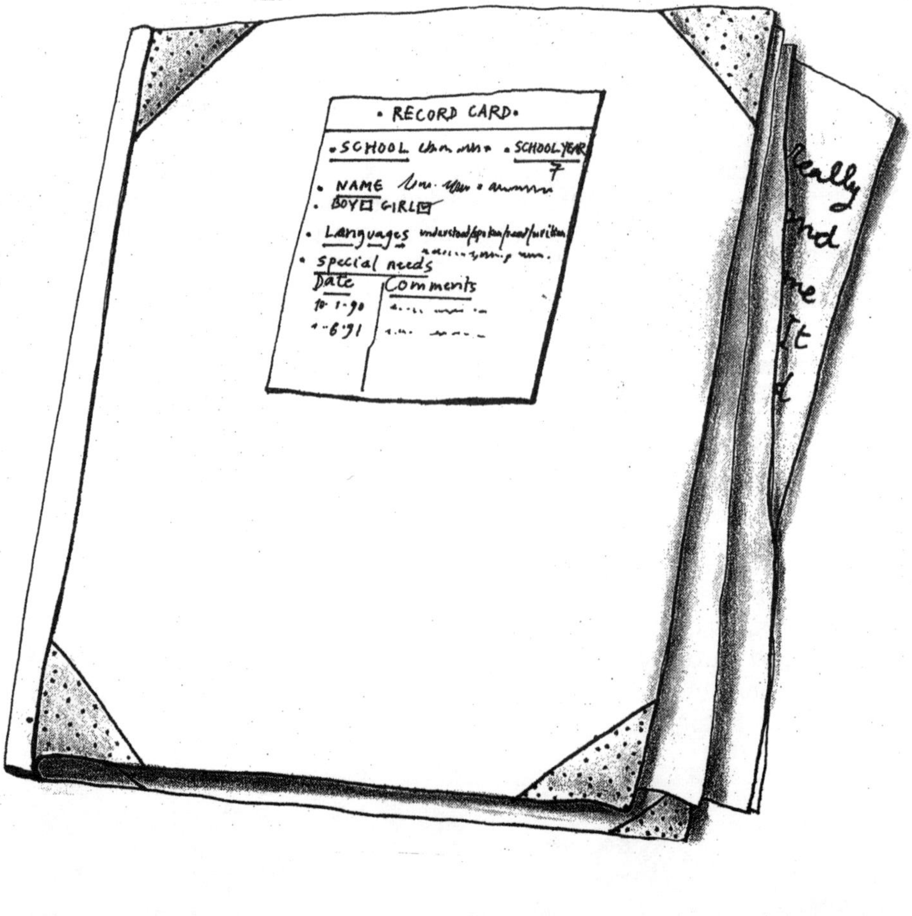

The wider life of a secondary school

The curriculum is central to the life and work of a secondary school. However, a school is made up of more than just the subjects that the pupils are taught. It is a community in its own right (sometimes quite a large one) with lots of other things happening at school. It will have a sense of identity, perhaps expressed through a school uniform, or through the way it does things like hold assemblies or welcome visitors.

This sense of identity can be fostered in many ways:

— **Out of school activities** Pupils and parents appreciate it when teachers lead other activities such as sport or music. Many talents can be fostered in a different environment to the day classroom and a sense of well-being, responsibility and belonging are encouraged.

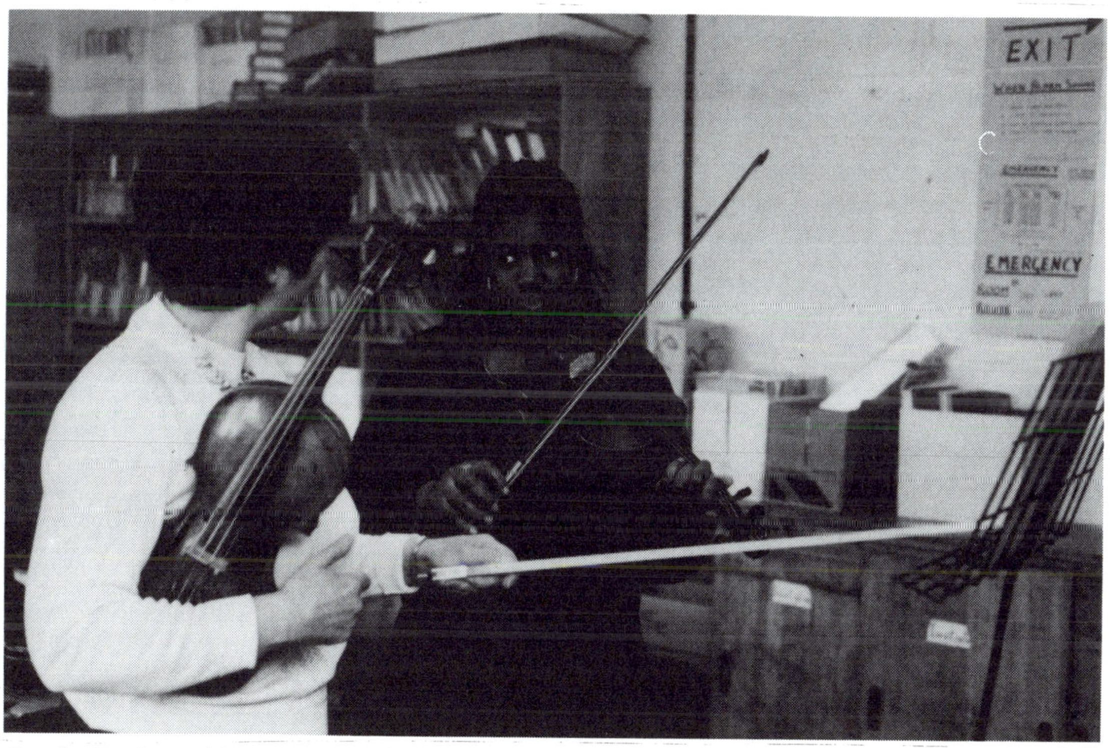

Good schools provide extra-curricular activities for pupils

— **Celebrating success** Healthy competition is an important aspect of a good school particularly when it is done in such a way as to encourage the best in all. Public recognition of success from a year tutor, or even a head teacher, help to promote an encouraging and motivating atmosphere.

— **The little touches** How welcoming is the school? Is there a parents or community room? Do teachers make themselves available at times which suit parents?

— **Parental involvement** Secondary schools are generally less successful than primary schools at involving parents in all aspects of the school's life and work. However, a good school will have an active parents association which arranges a range of social activities for parents, pupils and staff. As well as being good fun in their own right, such events can help to raise much needed extra money for the school.

Perhaps the best indicator of healthy values within a school is in the way it treats its most disadvantaged members. Not all children can be academic high achievers. Some children have special educational needs and cannot progress through the work at the same rate as other children. The National Curriculum can be modified for such children or even made not to apply. However, it is much more important to see what the school does:

— Is there a written policy so that you can see the entitlements of pupils with special needs?

— Are such pupils treated as individuals within their teaching groups and not made to feel different?

— Are there additional arrangements for assisting such pupils, (e.g. through specialist teachers). If so, where is such support given? Are pupils taught within mainstream lessons or are they taken outside the classroom to be taught in another place.

— Are the achievements of pupils with special needs recognized in the same way as the achievements of other pupils?

Monitoring your child's progress

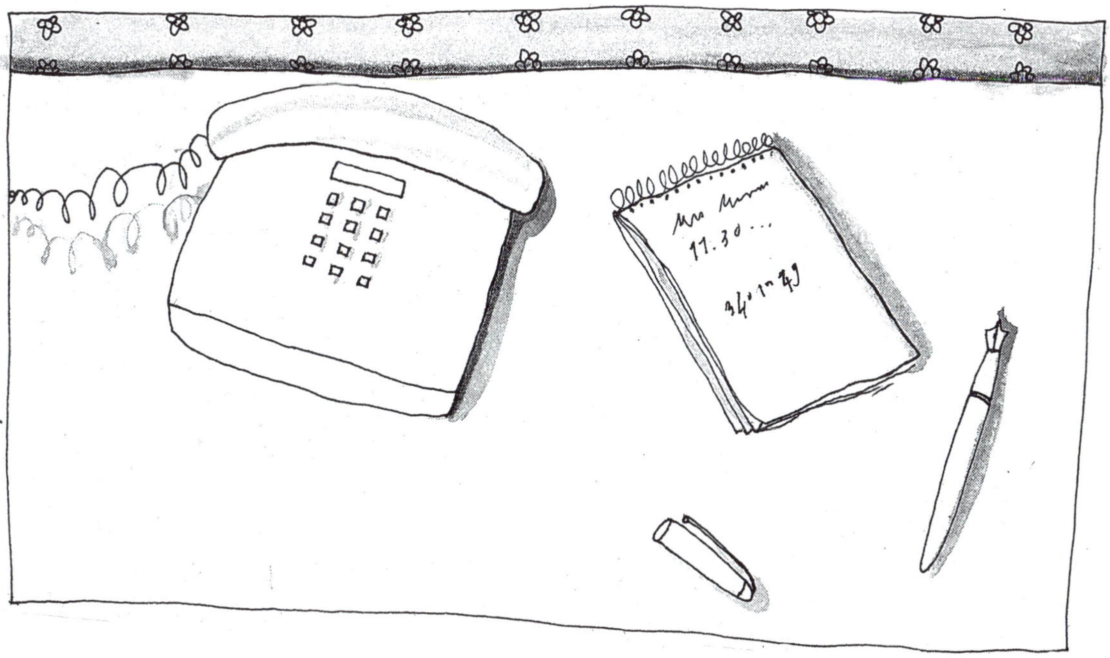

Over the past decade, many schools have seen the value of keeping parents well informed about their child's progress. Regular contact between home and school is essential if parents are to make sense of their child's progress through the National Curriculum. In future, parents will have to receive a significant amount of information about their children's work at school.

— **Programme of study** This is a note of the work your child will be doing during the school year. It will provide information about which National Curriculum subjects your child will be studying and what attainment targets will be covered.

— **Assessment information** You will receive advance warning about any assessment the school will be undertaking, both formal and informal. You will be able to compare your child's progress against the year group as whole and then look at the performance of the school against other schools.

However valuable written information is, there is no substitute for visiting the school and talking to teachers. The very best schools will ensure that the following arrangements are met:

1 **Regular access to individual teachers** This is the most important element of good communication between home and school. This may be offered half-termly, termly, or more/less frequently.

2 **A contact point between home and school** In most instances parents will be encouraged to use the form tutor as the first point of contact to discuss any issues that arise. It is important to know when this teacher will be available and how they can be contacted.

3 **Access to a more senior member of staff** In some cases, you might have to discuss an issue with a more senior member of staff such as a year tutor, deputy head, or even the Head Teacher. You need to have contact names and suitable times to call.

If you are unhappy about any aspect of your child's education, the first point of call should always be the one identified by the school. Most difficulties can be put right quite easily. Sometimes, you may feel it necessary to contact the Head Teacher or another senior member of staff.

It is very unusual for complaints to go any further but sometimes parents feel obliged to approach a school governor, who might raise the matter with the Chairman of the Governors and Head Teacher. If all else fails, the parent may decide to approach the local education authority (LEA). LEA's are required to have a system to deal with parental complaints about a school's delivery of the National Curriculum, such as a failure to deliver adequately a particular subject. In addition, most LEAs have an education officer who will deal with other complaints and investigate both sides of the story.

Friendly persuasion is more effective than complaint. An aggressively worded complaint can sour a good relationship between home and school, poisoning the attitudes of all parties involved. If you do complain, also remember to praise at the earliest opportunity. Teachers and Head Teachers are only human and they like to know that they are doing a good job which is appreciated by both parents and children alike.

Management of a school

The Education Reform Act, which introduced the National Curriculum, also made changes to the ways in which schools were managed. Head Teachers remain responsible for the day-to-day implementation of the curriculum and other aspects of the care and welfare of the children. Along with the governing body, they have a range of other duties and responsibilities which include:

— Overseeing the curriculum and conduct of the school
— Appointment of staff
— Discipline and attendance
— Financial management

In this last category, the Education Reform Act gave them significant new powers to manage and control the school's own budget. This is called local management of school (LMS). In the past, the local education authority decided issues such as: how many staff the school should have; how much money should be made available for books and equipment; and what aspects of internal and external maintenance of the building should be undertaken. Now, this responsibility lies with the governors. Money is delegated out to the governing body by the LEA through a formula; mostly allocated according to the number of pupils there are in a school. When the money is given to the governing body, it is free to spend it as it wishes.

Most schools have a school development plan which sets out its aims and objectives and its practices for the future. The governors will use this to decide issues such as: how many staff to appoint; what new books to buy; or what part of the building to paint. Under LMS, schools are being encouraged to develop their own sense of identity and go into competition with each other. Although this is happening in some places, many schools see the value to their staff and pupils in working in partnership with neighbouring schools.

The LEA retains significant powers, however. It remains the employer of staff. It has responsibility to provide adequate schools in its own area and manage capital programmes. Furthermore, it has the important responsiblity of monitoring the quality of teaching in schools, which is an important safeguard for parents, pupils, staff, local councillors and community charge payers.

The Education Reform Act also allows secondary schools to opt out of LEA control. To date, a number of secondary schools have done this either for what they believe are good financial reasons or because they disagree with aspects of LEA policy, perhaps wishing to be free of certain services provided by the LEA. Opting out is a major step for a school to take. Either the parents or the governors can initiate such a move before the matter is put to a secret ballot of all the parents.

Getting involved

So, how can you get involved?

— **Make contact** Find out who your governors are, particularly your parent governors. They will be a useful source of information and can be found in the school prospectus or the governors annual report to parents.

— **Become a governor yourself** Elections for parent governors are held every four years. Occasionally, vacancies come up or the governing body may wish to co-opt other people into its ranks. They are usually particularly interested in local businessmen or other people (including parents) who contribute to the community in different ways.

Being a governor will probably involve you in attending three or four full governors meetings during a school year. You may well need to attend some sub-committees, as many governing bodies have created these to deal with things like the curriculum, financial issues or the state of the repair of the school's buildings. In addition, you will need to visit the school regularly, to talk to staff and pupils, so that you are aware of all that is going on. Governors can also assist a school by attending its various functions and social events.

Moving on from key stage 3

The end of key stage 3 is an important time for your child since subject choices have to be made. The National Curriculum will ensure that your child continues with all ten core and foundation subjects until 16 years of age. However, there will be other options such as studying a second modern foreign language or following a dual science course. There are also options for pupils who may not be able to cope with the pressures of academic examinations such as the GCSE. Secondary schools provide plenty of information to parents and pupils alike before such choices are made. You will be given every opportunity to discuss the possibilities with your child's teachers. However, the vast majority of schools will try to ensure that all pupils undertake some courses leading to the GCSE.

The General Certificate of Secondary Education (GCSE) is designed to be taken by pupils of all abilities. Grades A to C are likely to be achieved by the more academic pupils, approximately 20 per cent of the ability range. Grades D to G will be achieved by pupils of all abilities and they represent a level of competence. An interesting feature of the GCSE is that the final grades are made up of a combination of formal examinations and course work. The latter element is likely to be approximately 20 per cent or 30 per cent of the final work. You have an important role to play therefore in assisting your child's progress as you need to encourage them to do their course work to the highest possible standard and ensure that it is submitted on time.

By 1994, it is hoped that GCSE grades will reflect a level of attainment within the National Curriculum on the following scale:

GCSE grade	National Curriculum level
A	10
B	9
C	8
D	7
E	6
F	5
G	4
U	3

Case study

From primary to secondary school

Schools try to make the transition from primary to secondary school as easy as possible for children and their parents. Here are some of the ways in which this is done:

— Regular cross-curricular meetings are held involving staff from all primary and secondary schools in the area. This ensures they are all teaching along the same lines.
— In-service training days are used to visit local primary schools enabling the secondary teachers to teach alongside the primary teachers. Sometimes a primary and secondary teacher will share a lesson and 'team-teach'.
— Teacher swaps are arranged between primary and secondary schools in the same area.
— In their first year at secondary school, students are placed in classes which take account of family and friendship groups.
— New students and their parents are invited to the school for a short interview with the student's form tutor. This helps put them at ease and familiarizes them with both the tutor and the school.
— Regular parents evenings, conducted according to class groups, enable the parents of students in the same class to meet.
— In the July prior to joining the secondary school, the prospective new pupils are invited to a school day. They have an assembly to meet the Head Teacher, are taught a few lessons in 'new' subjects (such as science in a laboratory or technology in a workshop), have a school dinner and are given a tour of the school.
— During the summer holiday, new children are invited to join holiday clubs held at the secondary school. Parents are invited to go along to help or participate.

The National Curriculum

Here are some of the ways in which schools are responding to the demands of the National Curriculum:

— Due to the extra demands that the National Curriculum places on school equipment and other resources, teachers might sometimes teach a specific topic (e.g. electricity, in science) across the entire key stage 3 age – range rather than according to year groups.
— A self-help group run by parents, and supported by the school, identifies and discusses parental needs and how they might be met. Members of staff often speak at these groups and the group sometimes asks the staff to produce leaflets giving important information, (e.g. about key stage 3). The group also sets up task forces to look into and report back on specific issues.
— Regular inter-departmental meetings are held to discuss the implementation of the National Curriculum. This builds on existing good practice within the school.

Schools are currently setting up assessment systems for their key stage 3 students. A variety of approaches are being piloted. For example:

— Folders of students' best work are kept as records of achievement up to age 14.
— Diagnostic monitoring is used so that all students are given help where and when it is needed. Each department aims at a quick, efficient and accurate monitoring system.
— Computer database assessment systems are being trialed. Typical categories of assessment are: standard of work; effort; behaviour; dress; and attendance. Systems give an instant cross-curricular view of each student's progress.
— The Government has decided that mathematics and science will be assessed at the end of key stage 3 in 1992. Schools may be advised to resort to 'simple' pen and paper written tasks at a designated time in the school year.

They enable teachers to keep parents informed regularly and easily. It is hoped that such systems can be adapted to handle key stage 3 records.

School images

Schools should work hard to maintain a friendly and caring image. The following are some of the ways in which this is done:

— Operating an open-door policy, where parents are free to visit the school at any time without making an appointment. They can even attend and observe lessons.
— Providing a parents' meeting room.
— Sending out regular reports and holding parent open day where parents are invited to visit at any time of day during a specified week.
— Encouraging parents to become parent governors and take on responsibility within the school.
— Providing a social centre for parents to seek help with domestic problems. Counselling and advice on educational and social matters is provided there by social workers, educational psychologists, Alcoholics Anonymous, RELATE, local churches and so on.
— Encouraging open-forum discussions of issues such as adolescence, drug abuse, vandalism and teenage pregnancy. This enables parents to voice their fears, share problems and obtain advice within a supportive group framework.
— Encouraging after-school clubs, societies and sports where parents and younger siblings are invited to participate.

Special Educational Needs (SEN)

All schools have SEN teachers who work alongside other members of staff to help cater for special educational needs. They work within the school in a number of ways:

— SEN teachers 'team teach' with regular teachers within regular lessons so that children with special needs do not have to be withdrawn to separate classrooms.
— All teachers have access to primary school records so that specific needs can be identified and catered for from the outset.
— SEN teachers teach at least one whole class lesson a week in order to be fully aware of the capabilities, progress and changing needs of all students.
— SEN teachers operate schemes to attract truant students back to school. These students are taught 'one to one' in their favourite subject until self-confidence is raised to a level where they are ready to rejoin their class.
— Students for whom English is their second language are given extra help in learning English. Their parents are also offered help with such things as form-filling and correspondence in English.

Conclusion

Many schools, despite a positive attitude, are concerned about a number of areas of the Education Reform Act 1988. One such worry is how the Local Management of Schools (LMS) will affect their financial situation. Since funds are now allocated according to how many students are on the school roll, schools are anxious about how they will finance large projects (such as the buying of computer equipment), how they will provide in service training for their teachers, and so on. There is concern that parent governors are possibly being over burdened and that new parents might therefore be discouraged from getting involved. LMS has meant an increased administrative workload; many teachers will thus spend a good deal of their time on non-teaching duties. However, schools have adopted a positive attitude to the demands of the Education Reform Act, including the National Curriculum, so that they can build with confidence on current good practice.